Soul Man

Soul Man

Five-Million Difficult Steps to
Physical and Spiritual Health

Tom Hafer

To order additional copies of this book, contact:
Xlibris
1-888-795-4274
www.Xlibris.com
Orders@Xlibris.com
737409

Contents

Before Becoming the Soul Man

Life is a puzzle, isn't it? Many of us have decided that our puzzle might be too hard, too many pieces. We wish we had the box cover to look at so we can see a glimpse of what our life is supposed to be. But we don't have the box. We assemble the scattered pieces the best we can, hoping we are doing "life" correctly and efficiently.

There is great wisdom deep in the souls of peaceful folks who have been successfully working on their puzzles for a lot longer than us. Their wisdom is this: *Don't force the pieces together. If it doesn't seem to fit, remain calm and try a different piece. It eventually all fits together as designed. Trust the designer.*

When we see our physical life through a spiritual lens, the puzzle pieces fit together perfectly. We learn to harmonize with the ebb and flow of life and we experience a cooperative strengthening of body and soul. Chronic physical conditions, anxiety, and restlessness are no longer the norm for us. We are well.

That being said, you can say my unusual story you are about to read is the synergy of spiritual and physical wellness in five million difficult steps. The "five million steps" is a rough approximation of the total steps it takes a hiker to complete the Appalachian Trail from Georgia to Maine. The long journey on America's most famous nature trail might be the perfect metaphor for a disciplined life, both physically and spiritually.

Personally, I have been hiking sections of the Appalachian Trail one week out of every summer since age fourteen. I have always found solace there. At the same time, every hike had consistently tested the limits of my physical capacities.

When I first started hiking the trail as a teenager, it was for the sheer thrill and adrenaline of the journey. Many miles of beautiful undisturbed landscapes and interesting little villages set the picturesque scene for each week long adventure. As I matured over the summers on the Appalachian Trail, my adventures became pilgrimages of sorts; spiritual journeys *to* God. Today, I don't see the trail as a path *to* God as I once did. Now, I see God as a travel companion; all the while, He is teaching me, quieting me, and revealing to me all the good and gracious things I missed before awakening to His presence along the journey.

This story is about the lessons revealed to me when I hiked the entire Appalachian Trail over a near six-month period in 2003. This was the year I became the "Soul Man". I hope you find that the lessons I learned are lessons for each and every one of us because we all desire - to some degree - a clearer path. All of us wish to cast aside our heavy burdens to travel lighter. We all want life's puzzle pieces to fit together perfectly. Everyone desires a life of *peace*.

When at peace, we have no worry, no resentment or bitterness, no jealousy or anger – and even our language has no forced, condescending, or aggressive tones. When at peace, our expressions are in harmony with our hearts, and encouraging words flow effortlessly like honey from the tongue. We exude positive energy. This positive energy allows others to warm-up in our glow. In time, we change the world around us on the outside if we remain at peace inside.

Don't force the pieces together. If it doesn't seem to fit, remain calm and try a different piece. It eventually all fits together as designed. Trust the designer.

Let me give you a little background into my unusual life. It will help explain what brought me to the trail in the first place. Let's start at the beginning.

I Was No Superman

I thought I was crazy for a very long time, but that was before I understood my *superpower*. Now I know I am not crazy, I just have a gift. Sometimes gifts don't make life any easier, in fact, I have read enough comic books as a kid to know superheroes saw their superpower as both a curse and a blessing until they discovered their gift was intended to save humanity, or Gotham City, or a galaxy *far far* away.

I say *superpower* as if I am some kind of Superman that can fly or lift cars and other heavy things, but that is all make believe stuff. This is real.

I think it is fair to say that you have some sort of superpower. Not flight or web spinning, but certainly you are more gifted at something more so than everybody else.

My childhood friend Ron had the power of super-hearing. Ron was a member of my Junior High gang. We were an inseparable foursome. Ron could hear trains coming a minute before the rest of us. We always thought he was crazy, too. Many times we walked the train tracks to the clubhouse we had built with scrap wood just outside of our little hometown. He would yell "get off the tracks a train is coming!" Bobby, Sean, and I could not hear it right away, but we did a minute later.

Ron's mom told us he had some extra ability to hear and feel vibrations or something. It was a handy superpower to have when he played hide and seek. He somehow always had one up on us knowing our hiding places. It was like he could sense our breathing, or feel our heartbeats, or even hear us pass gas from *far far* away. Quite a useful gift, it was.

It was most handy when we started our teenage neighborhood crime spree the first week of summer after seventh grade. The crime spree was short-lived. It lasted a week. In fact, we only stole three times and it was the same convenient store every time. It was the only convenient store in town. Our week of crime came to be known as the Great Candy Heist, and it happened like this:

- First, the four of us would go into the store. Ron - our super hearing friend - would go to the counter and ask for cigarettes for his mom (back then they sold them to us kids if we said they were for our parents, at least in our tiny trusting town).
- Second, as the cashier would turn his back to reach for the cigarettes, the three of us would fill our pockets with the two-cent gumballs and Hershey's Kisses. When the cashier turned around again, we would stop stealing.
- Finally, Ron would pay for the cigarettes and we all walked out together. Bobby, Sean, and I had our pockets full of stolen candy.

Simple enough? It worked like a charm. Ron was our secret weapon. He would be positioned by the front and only door into the store to listen for approaching shoppers who might come in during the time of the crime. His signal to us was clearing his throat if he sensed someone coming.

The first two times worked like magic. Then we got greedy. On the third robbery, Ron asked for cigarettes - the cashier turned his back - and right away Ron's bionic ears sensed oncoming footsteps. He cleared his throat but we were not paying attention. We were too busy packing our pockets. We got caught. Oh boy!

One thing about growing up in a small town - it was wonderful to have so many adults looking after you - unless you are a criminal. Word got out about the Great Candy Heist because everyone in town frequented that store. Heck, Mr. Herzog - the cashier - was my neighbor. We were shunned by every household. Our parents split the four of us boys up for the rest of the summer. No more crime. No more hiking to the fort on the train tracks. Summer was over for us before it even started.

About the time eighth grade was coming around in the fall, the town's forgiveness was setting in and the four of us began to hang out together again.

I think most people forgot about our crime spree by the first day of school. I can say it definitely cured us of having a future in illegal activities. I hated being shunned by adults all summer. It hurt. But, it was that summer I started to understand my *superpower*.

All four of us kids were ashamed in the beginning, but Ron, Sean, and Bobby seemed to recover pretty quickly. I didn't. I actually became physically weak off and on that entire summer. My parents were worried. The doctor couldn't pull me out of it with medications. I was just in a funk. But, the funk only came about when I was around adults from town who were disappointed in me. It was like a *negative energy* that people gave off. I was weakened physically that summer whenever I was around people who knew of the Great Candy Heist. At a restaurant, a store, even at church - anywhere people would gather - I felt their heavy disappointment, causing me to grow weaker.

Who would have ever thought the incident of the Great Candy Heist would lead to the discovery of my *superpower*? At thirteen years old I was going through more than puberty, I was starting to understand what made me different.

I know you probably want to ask me "what is your power?" Well, it's hard to explain because it is not cut and dry like the comic books. If you fly, you fly. If you have the ability to throw fireballs, then that is what you do. My power is different than those. My power is *a heightened awareness of the "energy" of others.* In other words, if you're happy or at peace, you give off positive energy and I get stronger. If you're anxious, distraught, or angry, you give off a negative energy and I get weaker. In simple words: *I can feel the condition of your soul* (I told you it sounds a little crazy).

Everyone has some degree of awareness of the energy of others, but the difference is I sense it exponentially more than anybody else does. It affects me physically.

Animals have a keen awareness of this energy, more so than humans. That is why your dog barks at people who are mean and wags his tail at genuinely happy, peaceful people. They can sense the "pheromones" people give off. It is really quite amazing.

Actually, *pheromones* are chemicals that are secreted in sweat and other bodily fluids that are more to trigger an interest in the animal of the opposite sex. It is how mates know the other is interested. It is nature's creative way to keep animal species populating. Pheromones also warn the animal of danger from another animal. My power is a lot like that. I can sense anger, anxiety, and hostility more than others. It has to do with what is going on in the mind, body and spirit of someone. My supersensitive soul detection ability is also compounded in crowds.

In a *troubled* group, I get really weak. The opposite is true. In a deeply peaceful or happy group, I feel overwhelmingly healthy. My body actually does get stronger (bizarre, I know). Like I said, for years I thought I was crazy; that is until I understood my gift. This *superpower* I possess had been a curse my entire life until I learned how to harness it in 2003 while hiking the entire Appalachian Trail. Now I use my power for good. I use it to help humanity. I can't save Gotham City or a galaxy *far far* away, but I know my superpower in some small way helps those I am around.

Depressed people have turned their lives around simply by me making them aware of the heaviness of their souls. They wake up! They become mindful of what is going on deep inside. I tell them they need to work out what is subconsciously weighing them down. If you need a soul repair, I will know it before you probably are aware of what is slowly stealing your health and peace of mind.

Stealing candy was not my proudest childhood memory. I got caught up in the thrill and paid the price. I never did anything like that again. I felt horrible. I could not shake the guilt from my conscience.

Our conscience does that to all of us. It keeps us from doing wrong because of the guilt we feel. Our conscience keeps us guided and honest. It also keeps us carefree when we follow its lead and make choices that edify our souls. Your conscience makes you feel guilty if you go against it. If I go against mine, I not only feel guilty, I get physically weak.

My mother just thought I was a sickly kid that summer of the Great Candy Heist. All that subsided when adults started to give me a second chance a few months later after the "heist" memory started to wear off. They did not have to say they forgave me, I could feel when they did. Their energy changed. I got my strength back. For me, negative energy was alike like Superman's kryptonite.

Careers

Through my young life, I was desperate to be around positive people in order to better control my *superpower.* I always found positive energy around people who exercised. I became a physical therapist so I could work with exercise minded people. This worked great for many years, but eventually I found lots of people with heavy souls obsessed over exercise as a way of escaping the emptiness they feel inside. I found that I did more good with these folks in spiritual counseling as I did doing physical therapy. In time, I decided on a second career to complement my first one. I went back to seminary to get a Master's Degree in religion so I could be a minister. I thought surely being a minister would surround me with positive churchgoers.

Of course in time, I found this was not always the case either. There were dozens of times through the years where I felt the collective troubled souls of gathered congregations. It helped me understand that *religion* does not always guarantee inner peace.

I found when churches spend time away from the pastoral comfort of scripture, the restlessness starts. Most of the Bible certainly paints God as a God of love and compassion that soothes the soul and gives us inner peace; but, some scripture paints God differently.

The churches where I experienced weakness had a lot to do with their ministers since they were the ones who decided which way to interpret God. They decide to portray Him either as a *comforting* God or as an *angry* God. If the minister was a genuinely happy and peaceful person, he or she interpreted Him more comforting. The happy minister's sermons were about a loving God. *Positive energy.* If it seemed the minister had an axe to grind, he would interpret God with that same axe to grind. His sermon would have a sharp edge. *Negative energy.* It made me realize that the religious leader who shouts a lot and loves very little is not as helpful to the gathered souls as the one who loves a lot and shouts very little.

My experiences in the churches taught me that the catalyst that drives us to have a peaceful soul is "love". It is what the Apostle Paul observed when he said: "if you do not have *love*, you are a noisy gong or a clanging symbol." With love, life does not seem to be a frustrating unsolvable puzzle. It is a guided spiritual journey where every puzzle piece eventually fits perfectly.

I remember visiting a church soon after I finished seminary. The members were having some sort of protest that was led by their angry minister. I really can't remember what the protest was about. There were fifty or so gathered people. They all seemed calm, but if you could have looked under their placid surface, you would have seen that they were restless. I imagine that their souls were like a flock of ducks. Ducks on the surface always appear calm and poised, but under the water - where you cannot see - ducks are frantically paddling their feet. The church members were like the ducks. They were calm on the surface, but something was going on deep underneath. I could feel it. Their defenses were paddling like crazy. Their souls were troubled below their calm appearance. The negative energy was crippling.

Now, years after I have claimed mastery over my *superpower* after hiking the entire Appalachian Trail, if I walk into a church and feel the negative energy, I warn everyone about the preacher's axe he is grinding. I tell them "most churches don't make you feel bad like this. Most churches make you feel really pretty good. You should try a different church." As you can imagine, this never sits well with the preacher who is already grinding his axe.

People deserve to feel good if they are taking the time to go to church, or synagogue, or temple, or mosque, or somewhere else to learn about God. I think most people want their souls repaired. Most people are searching for inner peace. It is when we are at our finest.

A life of inner peace means that everything is as it should be "inside" regardless of the chaos "outside". When you experience this peace, the puzzle pieces of life start fitting together effortlessly. Inner peace means you are not longing for a life different from the life you are currently living. You are not trying to arrive anywhere; inner peace is being fully present where you are, you have already arrived. Without it, our souls stay restless.

Like I mentioned before, I was always able to find strength and serenity since age fourteen on the Appalachian Trail; but it was my sixth-month trek in 2003 that taught me everything I needed to know to maintain my strength and inner peace at all times.

Before I tell you about the transformational wisdom that I learned while hiking, let me tell you what finally brought me to the trail in 2003 in the first place. I believe it will help you find your own inner strength and peace.

September Eleventh

All of us who were alive at the time remember vividly that September day in 2001. You will recall immediately after the unspeakable act of evil, everyone simply needed to play their part for the country's collective soul healing. There were no blue or red states, we were a "united" states. Blood banks had lines waiting outside so they could help victims. Prayers were being offered around the country. Parents hugged their children a little tighter. For the months that followed 9-11, we were on a fast track to unity. God's presence was not found in the tragedy. God's presence was found in the efforts that followed while we pulled together to heal the souls of everyone affected. In the face of pure evil, we did not turn to hate, but to holiness - to love – to heal us. The horrible tragic story that a few misguided terrorists forced us to participate in, was replaced with the epic love story that was, that is, and what will be tomorrow. We believed wholeheartedly in love's transformative power. In the church houses and other places of worship directly following the tragedy, so much talk was on finding the individual stories of 'grace' inside the tragedy. Jesus from the cross was quoted a lot, "forgive them for they know not what they do." There were so many wonderful stories of bravery from fireman and bystanders. It was a time of potential like never before. Like the sun's rays breaking through the clouds, it seemed that God's grace was shining through the wreckage and rubble in Manhattan. Like a new blossom out of the dirt, something beautiful was growing out of our broken hearts. Love was winning, not terror. If that renewal of spirit was to continue, many of us thought we could have possibly eradicated *hate* completely with *love* once and for all.

But, after months of healing, something started to shift. We began to forget about love winning. We collectively started to rely less on Jesus' words of forgiveness and more on our desire for retribution. We needed to even the score. We became aggressive against a common enemy. It wasn't long before we stepped away from the great love story and started to retaliate with another tragic story of *revenge*. Retribution was easily disguised as the next necessary step. Our souls were getting restless.

It has been said, "when you seek revenge, dig two graves." Violence against violence, expecting to end violence, continues to be a misguided logic that makes sense only when the soul is restless. But, when the soul is at peace, we can see revenge is just another step backward in the endless cycle of violence after violence.

After a brief time of healing following 9-11, we believed again in the folly of war to ease the ache of our restless souls.

Appalachian Trail

Because the souls of so many were aching, I felt I had to retreat completely onto the Appalachian Trail. It was the only place I knew I could get away from the collective troubled negative energy of so many people. People everywhere were like ducks, calm on the surface but paddling frantically below the waterline.

Sixteen months after the tragedy of 9-11, I chose to hike the entire Appalachian Trail. Somehow, I convinced Ron, Sean, and Bobby to join me. We started on the trail in April of 2003 at Springer Mountain, Georgia. For the months following, we made it to the northern terminus of the Appalachian Trail at Mount Katahdin, Maine. We finished just shy of 2200 miles north and east from where we started.

Along the journey, I learned life's puzzle pieces fit together perfectly. That seems to be how it works on a long journey of physical exertion coupled with deep spiritual contemplation; your rhythmic movement of your body allows your mind to go on autopilot and you get lost in meditation for months on end. Wisdom flows to you with great clarity if you allow the *busy-ness* of thought to subside and the *still small voice* of God to speak through the silence.

I journaled my near six months of meditation on the trail. I have decided the easiest way to offer this wisdom I have been given is to pass it on in its entirety without editing, mistakes and all. My fear was that if I try to doctor up the text at my desk years after the hike, I might ruin what was so clearly revealed to me. So, the remainder of this story is a raw copy of my trail journal I wrote years ago.

One thing that happens along the Appalachian Trail is a shedding of your old identity and naming a new identity, an *alter ego*. It is a little like the alter egos you read about in comic books. Clark Kent became *Superman*, Peter Parker transformed into *Spiderman*, Bruce Banner morphed into *The Incredible Hulk*; along the Appalachian Trail, I became the *Soul Man*. It was my "Trail Name" given to me by my oldest friends. As a hiker, your *Trail Name* identifies your new identity. All hikers get a Trail Name to replace their old name. Nobody tells them they have to take a new name when they enter the trail, everyone just does. It is part of the transformative power of the Appalachian Trail. It helps you identify who you are becoming along the trail.

So join my friends and I on the trail for the five-million difficult steps we took between April and September, 2003. It was the five-million difficult steps I walked inward to become the *Soul Man*.

Trail Journal

(Appalachian Trail 2003)

First Third: Fear to Grace

Springer Mountain to Damascus

Springer
Mountain to
Damascus

April 1 (11::15 a.m., day 1)

I can't believe we are actually doing this. We are being driven to
the Appalachian Trail from the Atlanta airport. It is a two-hour drive.

This seems to be a good time to put my first thoughts on paper. I figured I would explain the two incredibly tough discussions I had to have regarding my decision to "check-out" of life for six months. The first tough discussion being with work.

To convince the people you work for that you need to take a six-month sabbatical is not easy, I don't care how much they like you, it still requires a lot of negotiation. My bosses and coworkers finally agreed, I could use it. They were sensing that I needed to do something because of my physical and mental state. I was really lucky they didn't just say, "When you get to Maine, just keep walking," but I am a good employee. They won't be paying me while I am gone, but they are letting me keep my family insurance. I have their word they will welcome me back in six months. The good thing is I serve as both a minister and a physical therapist for them, so I have two choices when I get back. Wherever the need is greatest, they can stick me in either role. The place I work is a big senior community that is always expanding so I don't think I will have any issues in six months upon my return. Luckily, there always seems to be a need for either service I provide.

The other tough conversation, and certainly the most important one, was with my sweet loving wife, who lived with me and my ~~disabilities~~ ~~abilities~~ superpower all these years. She certainly was supportive and knew this was somewhat necessary. She will have to manage all the household without me, although lately I know I probably haven't been as helpful as I could have been because of being so incredibly weak and distracted all the time. My children - all three - were very supportive. They are fourteen, sixteen, and eighteen years old. They understand the lure of the adventure because I have continued the tradition of hiking on the trail with them each summer ever since they were old enough. They understand the adventure. They are cheering for me that I complete the journey. That is enough motivation for anyone to finish, I would guess. Even with their support, I am still feeling incredibly guilty about leaving my wife to take care of three teenagers and the house on her own in my absence. Luckily my two oldest drive, which helps with carpooling and grocery shopping tremendously. I feel guilty, but then I remember how important this trip is for the sake of all of us. Something has to change. I have to find an answer to my problem for the sake of all of us.

I have three companions who are hiking this whole trail with me, my oldest childhood friends. The four of us were inseparable. As kids, we did a lot of hiking together. We always said, one day – before we are too old to manage it – we would set off on a wild adventure that would kill us or make us stronger. We narrowed it down to two ideas. The first adventure was to canoe the entire Mississippi River. The second one was to complete the Appalachian Trail. We chose the trail. The timing seemed to be right for all of us.

To my surprise, when I called Ron, Sean, and Bobby, they said they will join me without a moment's hesitation. I know they sensed the urgency in my voice. Even though they had to have the same difficult conversations I did, they all said yes. So, the four of us are on this two-hour taxi ride to the base of Springer Mountain, Georgia. In the trunk are four backpacks. We have one emergency cell phone and charger, a credit card, a wad of cash, and everything we need to survive in the woods for the next six months. We are ready to take the first step of what will be millions of steps on the Appalachian Trail.

As we drive, I might as well say a little something about my lifelong friends. We were together since elementary school. We built forts together; they were also accomplices of mine in what was "The Great Candy Heist" 32 years ago. That was a pinnacle moment for me as a kid because that was the summer I realized I was different than everybody else. Other than my family, they are the only ones who really know about my hidden identity. Ron, Sean, and Bobby were a part of it all. It started with the candy heist. But, that was so long ago. They are so much more than one-time petty crooks.

Because of his superpower of incredible hearing, Ron became an engineer and audiologist and went on to patent a hearing device of some sort. I really don't understand what he invented, I just know he has done quite well for himself. He is tied down quite a bit. He does a lot of traveling and lecturing. That is what success does, the more famous you get in your field of study, the more everyone in your field wants a piece of you. I think this trip might come at the perfect time for him as well. He has plenty of money, he just wants the adventure.

Sean manufactures counter tops, "cultured marble", he calls it. He is probably even more successful than Ron. In South Florida where he is from, he is known as the "Marble King". He ships countertops, sinks, and specialty marble pieces around the Southeastern United States. He is free to do whatever he wants to do, and he is one to never miss a challenge.

Bobby was always into exploring, even more so than me. He makes maps now. He goes where there is no surveying done and he measures and records data, and makes the last frontiers known to developers so they can build. His company bought this big boat with a supersensitive sonar device. So now they are contracted by different agencies to map out the depth of the coast along the Atlantic Ocean and the Gulf of Mexico. I don't fully understand why or how, I just know when Bobby and Ron talk about this supersensitive sonar equipment, my mind shuts down. I can't follow. I do admire them both for the passion they have for their jobs and the expertise they possess with sound waves, I just don't understand it.

We ended up a diverse bunch. Our jobs are very different, but we all have amazing spouses and families. In a way, it made it tougher to leave for six months. But, I believe all four of us and our spouses knew it was now or never. We are not getting any younger.

Two of us had to ask our bosses and business partners for permission to go on this journey, but not Sean the Marble King. He just gave his "number two" guy a raise and said he will be in charge of operations for six months. And, Ron just didn't schedule any lectures or workshops until six months from now. His royalty checks from his patent are more than enough to feed his family. Bobby makes good money too, but he still has a boss. I don't make a lot, but we live well below our means. We always have. It is surprising how much money a family of five can put aside when they save.

It is truly great to be with these guys again.

Now, a little about this journal. I have decided that my entries in this manual will not concentrate on what everyone else is doing, or how much we will miss our families, etc. I am only going to use this journal for the insights worthy of documenting along the journey. I tend to ramble and if I let myself go, I would write a thousand pages and it would just be too much to read, let alone carry. So, I have opted to only enter my thoughts at times of inspiration.

The first step to any recovery is to admit you have a problem. My problem is I need to shed this negative energy that surrounds me and weakens me. I plan to walk right out of it. It will be like emerging from a thick fog to clear skies of positive energy. I will feel better, eventually. That is my prayer. That is the goal. Maybe along the journey I will figure out how to master this ~~curse~~ superpower of mine completely so I never have to feel so weak and unproductive again. That would be the ultimate goal. I think at this point everything I have is riding on me finding a ~~solution to my problem~~ way to harness the power of this gift I have been given. I feel this trip will either kill me or make me whole again.

Anyway, we are arriving at the base of the southernmost tip of the Appalachian Trail. Time to shut up and start stepping for real. Talk later.

(8:35 p.m., day 1)

We finished the first day hiking (Actually, it was only a half day since we did not start walking until noon). Oh my God! What was I thinking? I will never make it. I should have trained. I started the trail so weak. I barely made it to Stove Creek Shelter. We walked less than three miles after we finally reached the starting point at Springer Mountain. Only three miles on the Appalachian Trail today and that is all, 2,197 to go, give or take. I held my friends up terribly. I'm thinking they might be second guessing having to lug me along. I am so weak. We met a group of hikers tonight. The shelter is packed with them. Nice people, ambitious, but I had very few words, too tired to talk or write. I am having a hard time holding my flashlight and pen. (Goodnight).

April 8 (7:35 a.m., day 8)

It's been a week since my last entry. I almost quit several times but I am starting to get a "second wind". I am fifty-pounds overweight, weak, sore, and sluggish; but after a week of hiking, I am getting my stride. One day at a time, sweet Jesus. The guys are starting to see a little change in me. I feel like they are sick of me apologizing, so I decided to just shut up and walk. I have to make it. I thank God for their patience.

April 15 (6:45 p.m., day 15)

Found a stride. Another full week of hiking with no entries, no time. Met up with three other hikers. We are all moving fast. Over two weeks on the trail and we are close to Helen Georgia. About 50 miles on the trail already. I never thought I would say that two weeks ago. I can feel myself getting stronger and leaner each day, especially since we met up with these three other younger, faster thru-hikers ("thru-hikers" are hikers who walk all the way "through" from one and to the other, from Georgia to Maine). These six guys I am with all have a positive energy that certainly is affecting me for the better, too. I know Ron, Sean, and Bobby could not be happier since they are making up for the slow and rocky start. I continue to thank God for their patience with me.

April 21 (7:15 p.m., day 21)

My body is starting to change already from three weeks of hiking on the trail. I can feel myself getting in shape. In addition to having to tighten my belt a notch, my legs are not burning as much.

When you are out of shape, it is really easy to get a quick build-up of "lactic acid" when you are pushing yourself. Lactic acid is what that 'burning' sensation is in your muscles when you exercise with intensity. I feel it so much less frequently in my legs now than when I started three weeks ago. My muscles used to burn constantly. Now I just feel it when I am hiking up a steep hill. This is a good sign. I am being 'cleaned out' so to speak. During exercise, our bodies literally pressure wash clean from the inside out. Sweat and increased blood flow carry away stagnant impurities and toxins while bringing fresh oxygen to the muscles. This also initiates an orchestra of physical healing. *Lactic Acid* is one of those toxins that is pressure washed out of our muscles with fresh and clean oxygen-rich blood. This is why athletes heal so much quicker than sedentary people.

I am getting in shape; I certainly am not there yet. But I can feel a difference already. Thank-you, Lord!

April 30 (7:35 a.m., day 30)

This is the morning of our 30th day. We have now been hiking for a full 29 days straight. I haven't put in any entries for a week, it has been too exciting to stop. I feel strong, like a marathoner. I continue on with my old friends and the other three ambitious thru-hikers, and we were averaging 20 mile days the last three days. The difference in my endurance is ~~noticeable~~ incredible! I am stronger than I have ever been. I know the guys couldn't be happier. Finally, I am helping to set the pace. I am actually having to slow down for them. But, I certainly wouldn't tell them that after they have been so patient with me when we started a month ago.

We are 270 miles in already, even with an incredibly slow start. We camped last night near a town called Hot Springs, North Carolina. It is the first town since Springer Mountain, Georgia where the trail actually passes through town.

I have decided to take a "zero" day (That is trail talk for a day of no hiking). Everyone wanted to hike on, and I encouraged them to press forward and we will rendezvous at a town called Damascus in Virginia. They fought me for a long time on stopping in fear that I might not get there on my own without them. Secretly, I knew I could catch them fairly quickly if I had to, even being a day behind. I think my old friends sensed I probably could too. They can't believe the improvement in my stamina over this month. My oldest friends knew exactly what it was: positive energy. It is like Popeye's spinach to me. I walked out of the fog, now there are only clear skies. I traded the negative energy for positive.

I am taking a zero day, not because I need it physically, but because I desperately feel I need to take some time to put my thoughts on paper. The guys know I am trying to capture the inspiration while it comes, so they understand why I am taking this time to write.

We said our goodbyes and off they went this morning. I am just going to find a perch with a view and start writing.

April 30 (8:50 a.m., still day 30)

For the past month on the trail, I have been thinking about what I had been afraid of and what I hope to accomplish. At the pace, I am going and the way I currently feel – I don't have any more anxiety or fear about not finishing. I have been so strong and focused. I realize it has only been a month, but at this pace, I am going to make it!

The trail, the strength, the old friends, the new travel companions, the positive energy, it is all ~~good~~ ~~great~~ God's grace.

That's it... "grace". That is the word I was searching for to explain what I am feeling. This flood of positive energy is God shedding His Grace on ~~thee~~ me.

If there is one discovery we make that genuinely guides us towards positive energy; if there is one thing that strips away our cynical nature, our temper, our weaknesses, our anger or fear, it is discovering that we are ~~tolerated~~ ~~accepted~~ loved as we *are* and not as we should be. In religious language, this is *"grace"*. Grace is the unmerited and unconditional love God has for us. God loves the imperfect just perfectly. When we discover that there are signs of grace all around us, we soften our bristles towards others and learn to love them perfectly, imperfections and all. And, we learn to love ourselves, too. I am feeling the effects of this unconditional love. It is a flood of positive energy.

We should not mistake 'loving ourselves' as *narcissism*. Narcissistic behavior is filling your world with people to serve you. Under the influence of grace, you become 'selfless' and instinctively serve others. It is the opposite of narcissism. When we experience grace, we offer grace to others. We want to pass it on. My travel companions were helping and encouraging me even though they could have easily left me behind. This was incredibly *selfless* of them. All for one and one for all. I would not be here this far in the town of Hot Springs without their offering me grace.

Narcissists have big egos and only think of themselves. The bigger an individual's ego, the more difficult it becomes to be selfless. The ego fears shrinking. In order to grow, egos crush the spirits of others.

They steal strength from others. The ego gives off negative energy. I have been weakened by big egos all my life. But, selfless, egoless, grace-filled individuals lift the spirits of others. They strengthen me. My friends strengthen me. They give off only positive energy. Their energy is why I am no longer fearful of not finishing.

Fear holds us hostage, keeping us from reaching the harmony between our physical and spiritual lives. It is impossible to be a reflection of health while living in fear. A fearful humanity exudes negative energy keeping us all chained and paralyzed. It is what has weighed me down lately since we entered two wars after 9-11. On the other hand, grace unshackles humanity and mobilizes us in a peaceful direction.

Religious extremists are desperately holding onto their unchallenged religious practices out of their own fear of change. On a deeper level, they are protecting what is being threatened by a wider love story God is telling by His grace.

Terrorists plot out of their own fear, yet it is disguised as religion. Extremists stand firm in fear of change. Their only response is to inflict more fear. Violence becomes the end stage of this collective fear. Everyone suffers. Everyone experiences negative energy.

You can see what happens when fear enters the hearts of the religious. Out of fear we become cynics of the power of grace. In fear, humanity is divided. We become mistrusting of our neighbors. That is why terrorists are only effective if we become terrified. We stop making unified decisions for peace. We react out of fear and start stepping out of sorts and losing our firm foundation we once had through grace.

Jesus intended a grace-filled, fearless, selfless humanity. This was why he said everything in religion hangs on this understanding: *love God and love neighbor as yourself.* We forget this bedrock teaching when we live in fear.

Terrorists spread fear to the masses far and wide, like a manure spreader to the farmer's field. In the field where manure is being flung, there are seeds of grace, which are houses of worship, hospitals, Hospices, orphanages, homeless shelters, to name a few. These are seeds with the potential to grow into a healthier, more compassionate, selfless, fearless, and grace-filled future. We either tend to the seeds or tend to the fear. If we tend to the seeds, eventually grace will fill-up the field completely with positive energy. If we tend to the fear, negative energy grows.

When we decide collectively that a future of continued fear is not good enough for our children, we can use fear to springboard towards something better by nurturing the seeds of grace. Fear cannot survive in a fertile field of grace. Fear disappears in the presence of grace.

I am reminded of a riddle that demonstrates this:

Fear knocked frantically on the door.
Grace opened the door.
There was no one there.

Historically, corrupt religious leaders find God's grace too vast, too freeing, and too accessible. Loving God and loving neighbor cannot be corrupted. The corrupt lose control without imposing laws, doctrines, and dictums. Limiting the free gift of grace by building a wall around it assures access only through the attended gate in which the corrupt religious leader can monitor. This certainly is not the intended church. The church is not a building. It is the people, free and selfless. They just happen to meet in a building.

Clergy from all religions who whisper of God's grace inspire communities to be peacemakers. But, corrupt clergy shout divisive sound bites spreading a fear-filled prejudice agenda disguised as religion. One group nurtures the seeds of grace, the other group spreads the manure. God's grace is found in the calming whispers, not in the divisive shouts (Taking a break, be back later).

(2:15 p.m., still day 30)

I meandered into a pizza place in town for lunch, met a wonderful couple with a little baby. They inspired me to continue this morning's discourse on fear & grace and God speaking through whispers. So, I made up a story:

A powerful proclamation of God's wrath can be heard thundering through a massive place of worship complete with the angry preacher's shouts and pounding fists. Fear penetrates the gathered hearts. Next door is a much smaller older building - a terribly underfunded hospital birthing suite. Inside you can hear the cooing of a new life, just moments after its arrival. Huddled by his mother's side, the new life fixates on her silhouette for the first time while the exhausted new mother lovingly gazes over the shape of her child she labored into the physical world. Both mother and child somehow recognize, whether consciously or unconsciously, that God speaks louder through cooing than shouting. Grace is found in calming whispers, not divisive sound bites (The End).

(I am taking another break. I cannot stop thinking about that pizza place in town).

(6:30 p.m., still day 30)

I went back for a second visit to that same restaurant in town. I ate my second large vegetarian pizza myself and three side salads. The one thing you do more than walk while you're on the trail is eat! I am only a month in and I don't know how much weight I lost but my belt is tightened two notches already because of the extra 5000 or so calories I burn hiking eight to ten hours a day. Pizza is such a welcome change, I had to go a second time today. Our meals on the trail are the same. They are some combination of peanut butter, raisins, noodles, tuna packets, nuts, instant oatmeal, and any other instant high caloric food we can ingest. We also do a lot of grazing for wild blackberries and blueberries. After a month of the same menu, pizza never tasted so good.

While I was gorging for a second time today, I thought more about the day's journal entries on fear and grace.

It occurred to me "why" corrupt religious leaders abandon eternal hope of God's grace and use the more immediate motivator, fear. Fear can quickly rally troops in a pinch. It is easy to rally around a common enemy. But, it will always move the religious focus from love to judgment. With judgment, battle lines are drawn and energy shifts from positive to negative.

I once knew a minister who preached *judgment*. He met a desperate man with a drug addicted son, a kind woman with a broken marriage, and a scared pregnant teen. Judgment didn't work for them. They couldn't get any lower. Then the minister preached grace and they rose from their despair. Now the minister only preaches up, and not down. He preaches light and not darkness.

Grace is the light that shines on the footpath for people who have been walking in fear in the dark. In the light, the people who were once scared can plainly see that their path passes through green pastures and runs beside still waters. There is no more fear when you are walking in the light.

(8:30 p.m., still day 30)

One last thought of the day. As I re-read my own words on grace, I can understand how easy it is to become cynical about the nature of grace if you are one who experiences hard times.

I have found we all experience misfortune, some more than others. But, it really isn't about the difficulty of the current moment, it is how we process it internally.

The cynic experiences misfortune and blames neighbors and learns nothing while the spiritually healthy person lovingly shares with neighbors what he had learned from his misfortune. Grace's freeing magic only works when we are not afraid of being honest and genuine with each other. When we are free to share our troubles and lessons learned from them, all things can be used for good for those who love God and love neighbor. When you are not in fear of being honest, you assist others to not fear being honest, too. And, the truth shall set you free. And, the truth shall set others free, too.

If a nervous pew sitter remains paralyzed by the cruelty outside her church's locked doors, she remains a cynic, not allowing herself to believe in the ultimate transforming power of grace. A spiritually healthy person will fearlessly charge out the doors to the mission fields without hesitation. We evolve as a society only because the spiritually healthy members of society outnumber the fear-filled cynics. (That's it for this zero-day. Back hiking tomorrow. Good Night).

May 1st (7:15 a.m., day 31)

Good morning. I have decided to pick up the pace to see if I could catch my companions before the rendezvous point we pre-established yesterday. No time for entries, just going to hoof-it from here! Yesterday's zero-day gave me extra stamina! I feel invincible!

May 3 (7:10 p.m., day 33)

Two more days had passed since my last entry and I caught up with my friends! I can't believe I caught them already. They can't believe it either. Ron turned around after he heard me coming up behind them. I wanted to surprise them but those bionic ears did not let me.

I had picked up the pace to average 30 miles a day these last three days. This is almost unheard of, except for the extreme trail racers. My friends walked almost ninety miles in four days since I saw them, which is a very strong pace too, but I walked the same distance in three days! The truth is, it was more like a jog. I thank God for His grace that gives me strength.

May 15 (7:40 a.m., day 45)

It has been twelve days since my last entry and over the two weeks since I left Hot Springs, N.C. It had been the most beautiful views I have ever seen and I am happy to say the seven of us are taking a zero-day here in Damascus, Virginia. This was supposed to be the town they would wait for me to arrive, but I descended upon them in three days after my zero-day in Hot Springs. Here in Damascus, we caught the tail end of something called 'Trail Days'. It is an annual festival in this town where hikers gather to celebrate the lifestyle of the trail.

It is obvious that these folks at this Trail Days celebration have peace in their lives. The thru-hikers I have met already have given me an abundance of positive energy.

It is a good place to take a zero day. I am desperate to put my thoughts on paper again. I think we all earned it since we have traveled 470 miles already. We can afford it.

I thought of a clever story (Well, at least I think it is clever). It is about building bridges to neighbor's houses and not fencing them off. It goes like this:

A man named "Judgment" constructed a fence because he feared his neighbor. "Revenge" - who lived next door - was insulted and built an even higher fence adjoining it. The two continued building for years until the fence was impenetrable. In time, both Judgment and Revenge grew tired and died. The new homeowners did not know Judgment nor Revenge so they carefully dismantled the dense wall between them and with the lumber, built a sturdy bridge (Pretty Clever, eh?).

That story reminds me that all religions have sacred scripture that can serve as a bridge between us. For example, "The Golden Rule" - Do unto others as you would have them do unto you - is a solid bridge connecting all religions. A version of the *Golden Rule* was expressed beautifully by Jesus, Moses, Buddha, Confucius, Mohammed, Lao Tzu, and Krishna. This one rule - from sacred scriptures of all religions - offers hope in dismantling fences to build bridges. And the Golden Rule does not insist we all worship God in the same way. It simply insists we love our neighbors.

Today, religion is such a hot button. If the mere mention of interreligious dialogue makes a person angry or anxious, it is important for him to reevaluate why this might be. Has he missed God's grace because he is fearful of his neighbor's faith? Has he missed the forest for the trees?

We can fight over religion, reducing trees to sawdust; or we can marvel at the Creator's diverse forest that all great faiths hope to explain from different cultural vantage points. Sometimes conflicting views leave two religious camps shouting, neither one hearing. Both insisting on one way, missing the potential of a synergized better way where one and one is not zero, nor two, but exponentially more.

When our religion abides by the Golden Rule, we usher in a more peaceful future for our children. We treat others the way we would like to be treated. The Golden Rule builds bridges. As a rule, it can tear down fences between us.

My Christian education does not insist on its own legitimacy over the religion of a neighbor. The more I demand the world to see God my way, the less God's grace has an opportunity to work its transforming magic through me. In fact, the more I strive to be like Jesus, the more accepting I become of others. The more I am like Jesus, the less "religious" I am. I don't know what faith some of these hikers claim at this Trail Days festival profess, but they sure do emit incredible pheromones of positive energy. Grace abounds here at Trail Days.

I remember there was an elderly man in the nursing home where I work who chose singing over talking.

He said "people will argue with your words, but they will join you in your harmony. Words can divide, but music can bring voices together."

That guy gave off tremendous positive energy. I think he understood the spiritual life is a liquid, ever flowing, always evolving proposition perfecting us by God's grace. It makes me wonder just how much positive energy poured out of Jesus. It must have been truckloads. No wonder people were healed in his presence.

(Break-going to go check out more of Trail Days)

(1:15 p.m., still day 45)

I Spent time wandering around the food vendors at this festival. After scarfing down mountains of anything I can get my hands on, I realized how different the vendor-customer relationship is in this setting. The vendors are interested in the hikers. The hikers are interested in the vendors. They are truly building bridges. One of the hikers paid for the vendor's food with two paperback novels she was carrying in her backpack. Another vendor was giving out free samples and allowed people to pay on a sliding scale if they wanted more. I actually traded my water bottle and a tuna packet for a bigger water bottle with another hiker.

This different sort of economy is part of the "Trail Magic" that happens on and around the Appalachian Trail. The magic is about sharing, not acquiring. It is a different economy than the real world. It seems that mutual respect drives this Trail Magic economy more so than the money. Somehow everyone still comes out ahead.

This economy helps me understand why deep thinkers of all religious persuasions say our surplus of modern conveniences have not guaranteed us a happier and healthier future because we are also distributing record quantities of antidepressants and anxiety medications.

A surplus of money is never a substitute for what matters most. We know love cannot be bought, but for a moment, imagine this...

What if *love* was purchased with money? Not love of money, or romantic love, but genuine love for one another. Love that creates things like vaccines, child safety locks, and antilock brakes. In this new economy, like the Trail Magic economy, we would face a paradox because genuine love compounds interest quickly only when it is shared. It also dies on the vine if hoarded away. In this new economy, all people would rush to give away their love, their currency. In no time, all people would be wealthy – physically and spiritually – yet they would possess very little and their wants would be few.

Why don't we all just live this way? It seems to work for the hikers. I think we don't because of "fear", once again. we tend to hoard away our possessions because we fear we won't have enough. Fear of scarcity gets in the way of seeing grace's abundance.

The truth is, genuine love *is* the real economy. Money is just a vehicle. To understand this is to be truly wealthy. That is why these hikers seem to be at peace living with only 35 pounds of their worldly possessions on their backs for months at a time.

This Trail Magic Economy is a lot like grace. It is real freedom. I can't put a finger on why I feel so free. I just know the positive energy is electric! I have never felt this alive. It is all grace.

I heard the writer Phillip Yancey say once that God's grace can be dissected much like a frog, but the frog dies in the process, and the exposed insides are discouraging to everyone. I think Yancey was right. I read a small library about grace in seminary. It had cured me of ever needing to dissect grace any further. I quit trying.

Grace is best understood not with words, but by witnessing the liberation one experiences when he allows himself to simply accept it and then be effortlessly transformed by it. Grace is like letting go of heavy baggage that weighs you down. Maybe that is why hiking is such a transforming endeavor. You learn to walk away from the world's excess and just rely on three things: each other, the limited supplies in your backpack, and the natural water sources God provides you along the journey.

Just like this Trail Magic economy that happens spontaneously and naturally, grace is not ours to manage or control. We have no proprietary rights. Grace flows freely and abundantly like spring water. We are either hydrated by it, or we refuse to drink. We are not its source. We are simply the conduit to carry grace effortlessly downstream to others - from source, through us, to others. Trying to manage or control the abundance causes damming. Somewhere downriver someone will dehydrate. (Time for a break).

(9:30 p.m., still day 45)

I spent the rest of the afternoon and evening meeting hikers and vendors, swapping stories and singing campfire songs. What an incredible zero-day it has been in Damascus.

I thought this day in Damascus, Virginia had some similarities of the Damascus of the Bible. It was in the city of Damascus, Syria, where the Apostle Paul had his "conversion". The book of Acts said it was in Damascus that Paul was able to see clearly after being blind for three days. He saw the light in Damascus, Syria in the first century. I saw the light in Damascus, Virginia in the twenty-first century.

This place also made me think of my family a lot today. I gave thanks for a wife who is supportive and amenable to me ~~taking a sabbatical~~ "checking out" like I did for a life on the trail. I gave thanks for my children who are discovering on their own what God has in store for them. I gave thanks that I have the financial resources that keep the "home fires" burning in my temporary absence. I gave thanks for this "Trail Magic" economy that gave me real examples of love as currency.

I am optimistic about my children's generation. Most people participating in this Trail Magic economy are young people who still believe in the power of love, more so than the power of money. I pray these young people keep exuding their positive energy. I pray their Trail Magic mentality continue all the way through until they are old. What a world it would be for our children and grandchildren if that were so.

Today's Trail Magic made me think about a particular young single mother who works at our senior community. She is working for just above minimum wage in order to provide for her baby. She is often heard humming spiritual songs while taking care of the elderly with dementia. She treats the seniors with great dignity and reverence as they deserve to be treated. This single mom understands this economy of love. It is what gets her through. It empowers her to provide for her child. She doesn't get paid much but it is not the money that sustains her. The spiritual songs she hums are from her deeper sense of God's grace. In her world, love *is* the currency. Even though she has very little money, she is truly wealthy. And, something more is happening than simply quieting the sick when she works. In her presence, a veil is lifted that separates the physical and the spiritual worlds. Earthly groans of discomfort are replaced with a soothing voice. The spiritual bond that is created starts restoring body and soul of the sufferer, as well as the caregiver. Grace abounds. This is the economy of love. To be a part of it is priceless. (That is all for now. Good night).

May 16 (7:00 a.m., day 46)

Sun's up. Getting back on the trail, after yesterday's zero-day at "Trail Days". The seven of us are ready to blaze ahead. Probably won't be entering the journal in a while. We are bound and determined to get to Mount Katahdin before October 15th, which is the cutoff date to climb to the top. The weather becomes too risky to send hikers up after that, so thru-hikers always are mindful of that date and it keeps everyone pressing north. The way I am feeling after Trail Days, I could jog the entire way. But, I would rather hang back with my "Band of Brothers" (as the seven of us now affectionately call ourselves). My oldest friends and my newest friends provide the positive energy to sustain the way I feel right now. I am grateful. Even though we still have many miles to travel before we can say we are a third of the way finished, I know Damascus was a rite of passage for me. I saw the light. I spent the last 46 days on the trail not just shedding pounds of body fat that weighed me down, but more significantly, I shed my fears and purchased grace through the economy of love. Now I can say I am on a true spiritual journey, void of roadblocks. Ahead of me lay well over 1500 miles of trail, yet I am armed with my essentials:

1. My Band of Brothers.
2. My great health with twenty-five or so fewer pounds of body fat to carry.
3. A thirty-five-pound pack stocked with peanut butter, noodles, tuna packets, raisins, and nuts.
4. God's provisions of life-giving spring water along the trail.
5. But most importantly, I am armed with an insatiable hunger to *find* God on our journey. So I press onward. (that is all for now, heading north... peace!)

Second Third: Walking to God

Damascus to New York City

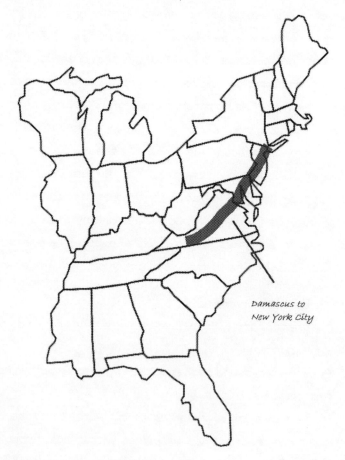

Damascus to
New York City

June 2 (7:30 p.m., day 63)

I have not stopped to write one time in over two weeks. We are

logging long miles with this community we have collected. Two older thru-hikers added to the four of us middle aged guys and the three younger hikers who have been traveling with us. Now we have nine in our *Band of Brothers*. We are hiking at a steady clip. We did 210 miles in twelve days, about 17.5 miles a day average since Damascus, Virginia. The pace is steady, but there is no complaining from anyone.

I am fighting the urge to take a zero day and write what is on my mind, but in doing that, I risk losing more days with my brothers. Even though I walk slower with them, I get much more out of the community that feeds me spiritually, as we work together towards our common goal of reaching mount Katahdin.

June 4 (6:50 p.m., day 65)

Half way through this day, we reached McAfee Knob outside of Roanoke, Virginia. It is the most breathtaking view to date. We are now 700 miles into the journey and 1500 to go. The nine of us spent an hour having lunch in near silence on McAfee Knob; silent simply because this view demanded our complete attention. It is beautiful.

As the guys got up to continue the hike, I bid them farewell, for I decided I have to take the time to meditate and journal. My words could no longer stay inside, I had to let them out. Besides, with the strength, speed, and confidence I have, I know I can easily catch up with them after a day of reflecting. Last time I was on my own a month ago, I had been able to travel up to thirty miles a day. That is unheard of; sort of superhero like, you might say. So I know catching-up with them would not be a problem if I chose to stay off the trail another day while my brothers hiked ahead. I have many things on my mind to write about; my church that I pastor back home, for one.

The community we pulled together on this trail made me realize we are a lot like a church. Our trail community formed an alliance to battle together the suffering of tired bodies and blistered feet. We assist each other in our tent set up and meal preparation. Through the common goal of walking the entire trail, we became a community, fully relying on each other. At its best, a church is a community fully relying on itself. Members lean on each other in hard times and celebrate together in good times.

They say living with a community of people who share life's ups and downs, adds an additional 14 years of life on average, when compared to someone who is isolated from daily interaction with others. Research labeled this phenomenon "The Village Effect". This might be why the church started so strongly the way it did. People lived healthier spiritually and physically, simply by being part of a loving community.

Today, those who are a part of a community recognize that the very act of serving others gives life its depth and flavor. And, serving others satisfies a deeper hunger that food, drugs, or alcohol, or other addictive substances never can satisfy.

A local church (or synagogue, temple, or mosque) contain a group of neighbors who gather together to discern God's hope for their neighborhood. Nothing fancy, just the body of regulars searching for spiritual food and serving each other by making sure no one goes hungry. I think D.T. Niles said it best, "the church is one beggar telling another where to find bread."

"The Village Effect" happens when we "actively" care for each other in the community. We can't care for each other from the couch. It is not something we can do during commercials. love stimulates our deeper yearning that is capable of turning off the television and bringing us to our feet. We actively support each other. Compassion empowers us to be the change in the world we hope to see.

We should never be impressed with the size of a church's membership. Instead, we should marvel at the calloused and dirty hands of its members who are busy making life better for everyone.

This kind of church is steeped in serving others. In other words, if a church is safely distanced from the world, its members' hands will stay clean while they worship in their ivory tower. But, the ministry will be reduced to "theories about ministry" and compassion will have no place to practice its craft. The church is the church when it climbs down from the safety of the tower, when its members roll up their sleeves and get their hands calloused and dirty. To say it a different way: when our religious walk focuses primarily on personal prosperity or pious practices, we keep our hands clean and germ-free. When our religious walk is one of a servant, then our clothes will get dirty, sweaty, and damp from the tears of those we serve. There is nothing clean about being a servant to others. The church should be filthy.

I know a church sometimes likes to be perceived as religious people who have it all together. Often, we hide away our weaknesses and struggles, denying the rest of the community of who we really are, only offering an avatar of our true self. We work hard on keeping up the charade. It is exhausting! But when we confess our imperfections and shortcomings, we wake up the spiritually healthy parts of ourselves and inspire others to do the same. Honesty unites. It is the only place to start on the trail towards real health: both body and spirit. We cannot heal what we don't confess is hurting. Grace insists that we share the pain as well as the joy with others. There is always the pain of childbirth before the pleasure of holding the child. The seed dies to give life. It is always night before the sunrise.

The church is built with flexible people with calloused hands who bend together but never break under pressure. Like a palm tree, the church will forever lean by the blowing of the storm's winds, but always to the side of compassion.

Our *Band of Brothers* functions like the church as it was intended, travelers assisting each other through the trail of life so no one is left behind. We serve each other, and in return, we all carry a lighter load. The church, synagogue, temple, or mosque is a *Band of Brothers* and sisters.

(It's getting late. I am sleeping right here under the stars. I am not even bothering to set up the tent. Good night).

June 5 (6:15 a.m., day 66)

Good morning. I decided not to write today. I also decided to take some more time to just sit in this stillness. I am observing today, and I will resist the urge to pick up this pen (Talk later).

June 6 (6:55 a.m., day 67)

I slept right on this rock outcropping. I slept like a rock on 'this' rock. I slept here two nights on McAfee Knob. I got up before sunrise yesterday at 6:00 a.m. and watched the entire day unfold as an observer. I meditated on this rock from sunrise to sunset taking another full zero-day just watching, no writing. I did not think I could do it, but I did. And it sure did give me fresh insight that I want to get on paper.

It is now a day and a half of zero days, but my soul will not let me leave this rock. I am transfixed by nature's beauty. Yesterday, all day, I found myself front row center stage watching the greatest awe-inspiring epic play of all times. At the first light of dawn, "Mother Nature" started her performance with her First Act. Her show was flawless. This was my critique:

"Mother Nature"

The dark stage was set early morning. The lights slowly rose from the east, stage left, because I was facing north. Over the slow and steady six-hour "Act One" that ended when the sun reached high noon, light gradually brightened.

While the lights were cascading across the mountainsides, the shadows of the tall pines and rock formations could not decide between light and dark. Light crept across the mountain faces, which presented a constant slow-motion kaleidoscope of reflections. The wind offered more fragmented shadowing by causing a rhythmic swaying of the trees. The shadows of the tall pines pointing like tips of spears. All spears stretched in unison pointing west at first, then disappeared at high noon, only to start pointing back the other direction throughout the Second Act. Wildflower color bursts were sprinkled throughout the lush green of the pines while white clouds and blue skies set the contrast against the earth tones of the mountainside.

The sun did more than provide light for the trees and rock formations to shadow dance. The sun also changed the thermostat to heat the open air theater. The warmth cued the orchestra – the early birds – to provide the music for Act One. The Blackbirds, Robins, and Wrens anticipated the sun, like a great conductor. As soon as the conductor appeared, they started their singing. The musical score lasted the entire epic performance in both the First and Second Acts.

In addition to the birds, the four-legged creatures had their part to play for the masterpiece to come alive. The animals danced incredibly fast compared to the slow movement of the shadows of the tall pines, but they moved every bit as graceful. No energy was wasted. All movement was filled with grace and beauty. Deer, rabbits, a fox, squirrels, and chipmunks, all had brief cameo appearances.

Mother Nature performed beautifully! I gave her a standing ovation at curtain fall last night. Her epic play did not disappoint. She has been the longest running show ever. She is consistent, yet always with subtle and exciting daily changes. Watching her performance, I am closest to God. Whenever I am weakened from the negative energy of others, I am refueled by her every time. She emits nothing but positive energy.

The small ~~stories~~ tragic-comedies we try to write with our own lives as the main character are pitiful substitutes compared to the Master's epic love story "Mother Nature", in which we all have a supporting role. To ignore her story is to pollute her perfection. We impose our small tragic-comedy when we forget about God's grand created love story He tells through *Mother Nature* – the story that was, that is, and that will be tomorrow. The story that selflessly ensures our survival.

Mother Nature is available to admire every day. Those who wish to take the time to watch her production will have renewed strength. But, seldom do people take the time. Perhaps because it is constantly showing, people seldom will see it. But, that makes it no less magnificent.

(12:00 pm, still day 67)

It is now high noon after ~~two full zero days~~ 48 hours of downtime. I virtually did not move except to stretch and to use the bathroom in two days! It was the least physical I have been in 700 miles. But I am ready. I have never been stronger in my life. I have 1500 miles ahead of me. My travel companions are on a two-day head start, but I still feel I can run for 1500 miles straight with a full pack. I am ready! I have been reenergized by Mother Nature. The trail is calling, so I answer. (I will write again, but probably not for a while. Peace!)

June 15 (5:45 p.m., day 76)

I Caught them! In nine days, after they had a two-day head start, I caught them! I practically was running. No time for an entry, but I am working out in my head what I am going to say to God when we reach Mount Katahdin. The obvious thing is "God! What an amazing world you created for us to explore! Thank-you! Thank-you! Thank-you!"

July 30 (7:15 a.m., day 121)

45 days since last journal entry on June 15th. Today is the first zero-day since McAfee Knob. It is my first full journal entry in almost two months. I traveled an additional third of the trail without journaling. We are in a zone. I have a lot of catching up to do. Like I mentioned six weeks ago, I had been hiking alone ever since I left that incredible experience on McAfee Knob, but I caught up with my community after nine days of hiking alone. I have to admit, even though I averaged about nine additional miles a day on my own, I would rather be with my brothers any day. For the last 45 days, we traveled together. We have doubled our mileage since McAfee knob. We are now at Bear Mountain State Park, New York. We are almost exactly 1400 miles into our journey. We are two-thirds of the way finished with the Appalachian Trail; one-third to go.

Since I have 700 miles of thoughts in my head, I am going to take some time to unpack it.

It is funny, we never really think of it until we take a moment to reflect on how far we have come on the trail. It really is just like life. All of us work, yet we get lost in the day to day. I wonder how often the average person picks up his head from his desk and ask "Is this what I am supposed to be doing?"

If the trail is the metaphor for life, imagine being four months into it and finally asking the question "is this the direction I am supposed to be walking?" Imagine if we never consulted a map or asked fellow travelers 'which way is north?' Imagine if we did not look-up and see the white hash mark trail indicators on the trees? (they mark the entire trail. Hikers call them "White Blazes". There are a million of them).

If we didn't read the signs, or maps, or look at the white blazes, we could have possibly walked for four months and gone nowhere.

Life can be like that if you don't know what direction you are supposed to be going.

The nine of us decided to rest in the grass at the monument on top of Bear Mountain. From this place, you can see the New York City skyline. It is about 30 miles away. This morning it is a little foggy. You can make out the buildings of Manhattan, minus the twin towers. It is coming up on the second year since the tragedy. This place makes me think of the eight-million or so people who are working just thirty miles away in the big city. Maybe it is because I am two-thirds along the trail, or maybe it's because my soul still aches for New York, but I can't help but wonder how many of the eight million in the city feel passionate about the job they currently have?

So often we don't take the time to see the signs pointing us, nudging us, encouraging us in the direction we are supposed to go to follow our calling. So, by default, we just decided to work uninspired for the highest bidder. I guess I am talking about the trap of "busy-ness". Busy-ness is working without inspiration. It is watching the time clock and missing the value of time. Busy-ness sacrifices quality at the altar of production. If someone experiences prolonged uninspired busy-ness in his work, he should stop for a moment - remain still - then pray the question "Why am I here?" In time, he will be cured of busy-ness. His time will once again have value if he takes the time to look for the signs directing, nudging, and inspiring him to travel in the direction of his calling.

Humanity needs quality work, not more quantities of uninspired trinkets, widgets, and reality shows. Individuals who value their time produce quality work. Even Tolstoy said, "in the name of God, stop a moment, cease your work, look around you!"

One might think "if I retire, I would have peace because I would have time to do what I want." And on retirement, one often finds added anxiety, not peace, since he feels his sense of purpose is gone when the work is finished. No purpose, no peace. In my careers as a physical therapist and a minister, I have the privileged opportunity to know hundreds of seniors, many are one-hundred years old or older. If you are lucky enough to chat with a one-hundred-year-old, ask her about her life's work. She will be quite nostalgic recalling fondly the hard but honest labor, eagerly sharing how her once capable hands made a positive difference. She won't mention the money. She won't care. The earnest, valuable work itself was its own reward. Her sense of value is one of the reasons she made it to one-hundred.

If a child has earthly parents who engage in meaningful work, that child grows up perceiving a world that will benefit from his meaningful work, too. He sees apathy and entitlement outside the home, but a strong sense of calling and purpose from the adults inside the home. He finds his parents generate value with their hands and minds. It liberates the child to respond to his surroundings thoughtfully. He will look for opportunities where his gifts, his passions, and his community's needs can all fit together perfectly like the pieces of the puzzle. He will offer his gifts to those who can benefit from them. It will be his passion, his calling. He will actively offer his value to others. He will not suffer from any damaging feelings of worthlessness; nor will he fall into a belief that he is entitled to something for doing nothing. He will want to express his value to the world through his creativity.

At first, it will appear money might be the highest motivating factor. It is not. Like his parents, his motivation will come from the positive change he sees that he is capable of manifesting by engaging his gifts and passions for the benefit of others. The child sees himself as capable and needed, therefore he is valued and inspired. Money is just the vehicle that the world offers him in exchange for his inspiring work he offers the world. Like the *Trail Magic Economy*, love will be his real currency. He will exude positive energy. He will feel valuable.

(Taking a break. The sun has burned off all the fog. We can see the Manhattan skyline, beautifully. I think I will just watch it a while. I miss the twin towers).

(11:00 a.m., still day 121)

The entire trail, I thought of my wife and children, but I avoided journaling much about them for the sake of brevity. Like I wrote on my first day driving to Springer Mountain in Georgia, 1400 miles ago, I purposely wanted to keep focused and brief, journaling only during times of inspiration. I fought the urge to bring family stories into this journal to keep it concise, but I have to share a little something because family is to me the most important gift we are given and I would be remiss to not get a little personal.

I realize how amazing it is to have a supportive wife who understands my ~~problem~~ gift and knew I had to disappear into the woods to learn what it had to teach me in that regard. None of my children are ~~different troubled~~ like me. They are perfectly normal. They are not burdened with the negative energy of others like I am. I thank God for that. Yet, I consider them all superheroes in the sense because, like any superhero, the world is a better place with them in it. That is certainly true with my teenagers. I pray most parents feel the same way about their kids.

When our last child was born fourteen years ago, our doctor allowed me to deliver her. I was the one who gently eased her into this world. And since, it has been endless excitement of dancing, bad singing duets, and dreaming of what she will become. These are the rewards of parenting if we do our job.

"What is our job?"

I'm glad you asked.

Our job as a parent is as follows:

- to be present.
- to bring fresh air when life begins to suffocate.
- to be the eternal optimist even when you are weak.
- to attend 10,000 hours of sporting events, practices, and award ceremonies.
- Carpooling and chaperoning everything a teacher asks, because you know teachers have a shortage of adults to help inspire and lead the students.

These are some tasks of being a parent. We pay forward a sense of value in our children. They grow up knowing they are valuable. They will use their gifts and passions and navigate the needs in the world where they can best serve. They will work - not watching a clock - but with a sense of calling. They will grow up inspired. They will emit positive energy.

Our greatest hope as parents is to have our children stand on our shoulders, look at the horizon, and eagerly tell us what they see and how they will go about making it better for everyone. This is the difference between watching a clock and working inspired with a sense of calling. Taking parenting seriously is not just a gift to our children, it is a gift to humanity.

(I am going to take a break from writing for a while and check-out the area. We are thinking of taking a train into the city, not sure yet).

(9:10 p.m., still day 121)

All of us just came back from the zoo that is close by. We decided against the city. Most of us thought we would go into shock after four months in the woods. We would maybe feel too claustrophobic, too boxed in with all those people. So, we decided to go to the zoo that we could walk to from here.

It was interesting but sad to see the animals in cages. We saw the same animals running around free along the trail. It is easy to see why so many people say they feel ~~stuck~~ *trapped* in their jobs like they are in cages. Maybe the trail represents more than life; maybe it represents a life without cages. Even though there is more security in cages than out in the wild, cages are still cages.

It made me think of what the terrorists did to our country almost two years ago on 9-11. Sure we are safer now; we tightened up our borders, we started a Homeland Security Initiative, we beefed up the Transportation Security Administration (TSA), and millions more of the good guys now own guns and alarm systems. We are no doubt more secure, but we seem to be more "caged" than we were before. Maybe someday it will feel different. I hope.

The last thing we did on this zero day today is look out over the New York City skyline at sundown. We said prayers for the continued healing of Manhattan and our country. We thanked God for the good and great things we still have left to do and see. For today, the nine of us know that God had called us out of our safe cages to the untamed trail. It had something to teach us. What we do with that wisdom, well, that will be unveiled for each of us when the time comes.

Today, I thought of Henry David Thoreau saying: "I went to the woods because I wished to live deliberately, to front only the essential facts of life, and see if I could not learn what it had to teach, and not, when I came to die, discover that I had not lived."

That is exactly how I felt since I stepped on this trail 1400 miles and four months ago. We have lived deliberately, fronting only the essentials of life to learn what God has to teach us out here.

Last Third: Walking with God

New York City to Mount Katahdin

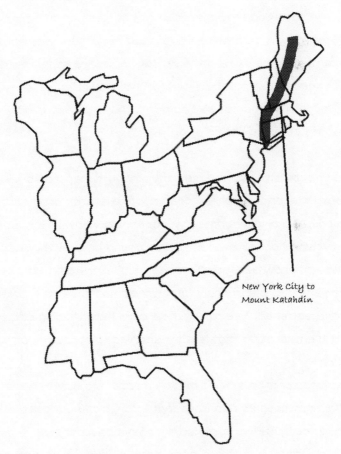

New York City to
Mount Katahdin

August 4 (8:00 p.m., day 124)

I was not going to write tonight, but I have to share this incident that happened on the trail today. It took place just north of the Appalachian Trail overpass that crosses highway 90 near Stockbridge, Massachusetts. I found out hikers need to be more careful with this stretch of the trail since it intersects many small country roads. Not everyone likes dealing with the constant flow of hikers in these small towns.

Today, I was crossing a street when two guys passed by speeding and shouting obscenities. I had to hurry up and get off the road to avoid getting hit by their car. It was apparent they did not care for hikers. The car skidded to a stop and both men got out. It looked like there was going to be trouble. My Band of Brothers was spread out pretty far behind me. I was not sure how far ahead of my friends I was in case I needed assistance. The men walked up to me; they looked pretty rough. They had an axe to grind, that was apparent. And you know what happened next?

Nothing.

I can't explain it exactly. I felt their negative energy but I did not get weak or scared. I sensed the negative energy and I simply took a pass on absorbing it in any way. I don't know how I did it, but I did. I found myself at peace even in this profound presence of negativity. The men somehow sensed my peace of mind. It was a little bizarre.

They shouted questions; I answered their questions. Eventually, their tone softened. We talked. The calm I was feeling diffused the angst in them, at least that is what seemed to happen. Violence was avoided.

My peace of mind allowed me the freedom to survey the situation since I did not have to deal with fear or weakness. I could see they were two young men who looked like they had a hard life. They drove an old Kia Spectra that had seen better days. Their clothes were old. They were terribly unhappy and mad at the world. Their souls were deeply troubled. I felt it. But yet, for the first time, I didn't absorb the negative energy. It was no longer my kryptonite. I stayed strong and calm.

After the diffusion of their anger, it turned out they were not bad guys, just misunderstood. They were brothers. One did not finish high school. They both used to work factory jobs until the economy changed. One was married; one recently divorced. One was thinking about moving south, but the other felt they should start a roofing business together. They both had dreams.

I stood with those men for an hour. I don' t know how it happened. I just know it was supernatural in a way. By the time we were finished talking, all my Band of Brothers caught up to me. The two brothers met all eight of my brothers. We talked. We encouraged. We laughed. We thanked them for their time. And, we all went on our way. They went back to their Kia; we continued north.

My Band of Brothers had no idea those two men approached me with anger. The two brothers had no idea how their energy changed inside of an hour, but it did. By the time those two men left me, they were emitting positive energy. I felt the change. They both decided they were going to give the roofing idea a try. They thanked me for taking the time to talk today.

They thanked me? I am still confused. I think they are, too. What happened? It is a mystery. A beautiful, grace- filled mystery (goodnight).

August 31 (9:15 a.m., day 153)

It has been a full 32 days since our last zero-day overlooking the New York City Skyline at Bear Mountain State Park. We are so far ahead of schedule, we decided to take another day and just relax and reflect.

Peace is all I have now. I don't really know where we are exactly. I don't really care. All that I know is I am at peace and we are traveling north; because, we have carefully observed the signs around us, guiding us, nudging us, and calling us towards Mount Katahdin.

I am a short distance from the end after five months. I am somewhere in the White Mountains of Maine heading north, and I am grateful, strong, and happy to be alive. The nine of us are two weeks ahead of where we thought we would be on this day, so that is really great as well. It means getting back to our families ahead of schedule.

My Band of Brothers assigned me the Trail Name "Soul Man" because they see me as a sort of spiritual guide on our journey since I tend to describe observations theologically. That is kind of what ministers do, we put a "God spin" on everything. But, only my old friends know about my ~~weakness~~ gift (sorry, I do that every time, old habit). Our five new travel companions have no idea about my gift. I never told them I can feel their soul, their energy. I didn't have to tell them. There was no negative energy, only positive. As far as they know, they just assume I am an incredibly gifted middle-aged athlete. But, the truth is, I was "energized" by the positive energy from them and all the other hikers along the journey. Clark Kent only revealed he was Superman when there were emergencies (Well, he never "revealed" he was Superman, he changed into Superman when there was a crisis). I remained who I am without revealing my secret. I know now there does not have to be a personal crisis. I can always remain strong and at peace. It is not the negative energy itself that weakens me, it is my response to the negative energy that weakens me. I know now I can either accept the negative energy or politely decline it.

This journey had revealed to me that my companion's positive energy is being replenished daily by a source. After five months in nature on the trail, we have removed the distractions that were keeping us from God. We are not walking "to God" as a destiny as I once thought we were doing. God is walking with us along the journey as a travel companion; All the while, He is teaching us, quieting us, and revealing His grace to us. This unlimited positive energy comes right from the source of all life, God, who travels with us. And, this energy flows into us, and effortlessly through us to others, as long as we remain open to this flood of positive energy called grace.

I am at peace with everything. I am in love with all that is good, twenty-four hours a day and seven days a week; And, when I choose to walk with God - I "decide" not to pick-up negative energy of others. I have learned this along the trail, along this long journey inwards. It took me nearly 2000 miles and five-million steps to discover that I always have a choice. I decide against absorbing any negative energy, only positive. I accept only energy that flows from the source of all life. We all have that choice.

Since the source of positive energy is of God, then negative energy is not of God. Negative energy comes from all over, just not from God. Negative energy radiates out of big egos that need to feed on others to grow. Negative energy emits from a narcissist who needs to devour what is good and hopeful in others. Negative energy comes from the preacher who has an axe to grind. Negative energy comes from the terrorist who resorts to violence because he fears the greater love story God is telling through grace. Negative energy comes from anyone wishing harm to anyone.

When we are in the presence of positive energy, we make healthy and mindful choices regarding our spiritual and physical health. When influenced by positive energy, we choose healthy relationships; we refuse harmful substances; we chose to share kindness; we choose to eat foods that will nourish us; we care for Mother Nature; And, we choose to take active steps away from a sedentary lifestyle. The health of body and soul is our choice. Alleluia, it is our choice to live well!

Peace of mind, body, and spirit do not exist because God demands it. Peace exists because grace - God's simple love story - has been moving hearts for millenniums. Kingdoms will rise and fall, yet our children and our children's children will have access to this spiritual peace simply by allowing their hearts to be open to God's unlimited grace. Life becomes a spiritual journey when we lose the notion that we are on that frantic foot race competing to find God. When we walk away from the "busy-ness", once the dust settles; then, we become aware of God's presence. We see clearly we were not racing to find Him in some heavenly future, God was and continues to be our travel companion in life in the present. This spiritual awareness of God's presence allows us to quiet our minds regardless of the negative energies that surround us. We maintain inner peace.

We sing, not shout.

We caress, not grab.

We share, not hoard.

We love, not hate.

The anxious person reacts to conflict in a physical way. The peaceful person's reaction is more spiritual in nature, not physical. The person at peace does not have to reason with aggressive speech and high blood pressure. The peaceful are comfortable in their own skin and therefore are not easily rattled by the negative opinions and actions of others. In essence, the peaceful calm the anxious. The anxious will learn to stay comfortable in their own skin as well. Collectively, peaceful people create a calm world to live in by reacting by *not* reacting at all. This is what spiritual awareness of God's presence does to us.

Imagine yourself in the boardroom...Imagine there is a lot of arguing. Everyone is anxious. Everyone's ego is flaring, demanding they be heard as the one and only solution. Clenched fists, tension headaches, and irritable bowels are everywhere, yet you still hear the gentle rhythms of the mountain breeze blowing through the trees; you feel the warm sunshine on your shoulders; you smell the fresh evergreens; you taste the ever flowing cool refreshing spring water. Your spiritual presence calms the physical storm others are experiencing. Those who were fighting to get their points across in the meeting exchange their egos and anxiety for peace of mind, just like you. You find more is accomplished in the next cooperative hour than anyone ever dreamed possible, thanks to your spiritual awareness of God's presence.

September 11 (6:30 p.m., day 164)

Eleven days have passed since last entry. We are just a few days from the terminus of the Appalachian Trail at Mount Katahdin. Today is the second anniversary of the tragedy in Manhattan. We have traversed an additional 650 miles since we were right outside New York City. Another prayer, another day of healing as we travel the trail towards its end. Although it ends in a few days, for me, it is just the beginning of a new life. I have complete mastery of my gift, my superpower. Negative energy has no more effect on me. I know God - the source of all life - travels with me. I control my own destiny simply by accepting the positive and politely declining the negative energy of others.

I know my gift is meant to be used to wake up others to the full awareness of God's presence. This potentially can cause a surge of positive energy in our nation, a flood of peace and healing for all.

It is time for our country to heal, to begin again. We can all collectively turn towards the positive and politely decline the negative energy around us. Eventually, everyone will wake up to the fact we are walking with God as a travel companion each day. We are showered by His grace.

September 13 (6:30 p.m., day 166)

This is the last full day on the journey. We are camping at the foot of Mount Katahdin in Baxter State Park at Katahdin Stream Campground. There are only six miles remaining and the journey is over.

The *Band of Brothers* is still together. Most of us have been together off and on for 14 states and nearly 2200 miles. I will miss them. But, I think the nine of us will always be friends. We have done something much bigger together than any one of us ever had done alone. Tomorrow we will hike to the end. We will celebrate one last night with fellowship and libations (most likely). Then, we will depart in solitude after nearly five and a half months on the trail together.

One of the things I was thinking about today as we prepare for the last day of hiking is this: when asked to point to ourselves, we don't point to our brains or stomachs, or diplomas or paychecks, we point to our most vulnerable place, the center of our chests. We point to our hearts. We instinctively tell the world "this is the heart of who I am. I trust you will be careful and not break it. I, in turn, will be careful with yours." It is the best part of all of us.

When a troubled person is forced into solitude, he grows more anxious since he is now completely alone with his negative thoughts. He has no way to diffuse his pain by imposing his hostility or destructive behaviors on others, nor can he utilize outside distractions or substances, like drugs and alcohol, to mask the anxiety and emptiness he is feeling inside. He is alone in his negative energy. That same solitude to the practicing spiritually healthy person, who desires only to rest with God, experiences nothing but inner peace and positive energy because he is finally freed from earthly distractions. The spiritually healthy individual finds rest in solitude. This is life along the trail, no distractions and only grace, a flood of positive energy.

Inner peace has no short-cuts and it cannot be hurried. Like fruit on a weather-beaten mature tree, inner peace is the fruit produced from a long disciplined spiritual journey inward.

September 14 (1:00 p.m., day 167)

It is finished! The weather was perfect. We hiked for the last time. We touched the Mount Katahdin sign. That was the final step of the thru-hiker who completes what he set out to do. The Thru-hiker walks nearly 2200 miles, five-million steps, one step at a time (truth be told our total was only 2176 miles, but who is counting).

It is finished!

September 15 (2:30 p.m., 1st day off the trail)

The nine of us spent our last night off the trail in a tiny motel near Mount Katahdin. At the only restaurant in town, we drank several celebratory pints, gorged ourselves, and swore off hiking, at least for a little while. I have a feeling all nine of us will periodically return to the trail at some time. It still feels surreal that we are off the trail after walking for 167 days.

I am writing on a bus on our way to the Bangor Airport with Ron, Sean, and Bobby. Soon the four of us will start to break up while we board our flights to return to our homes in four different corners of this great country. We said our goodbyes to our other travel companions back at the motel. We most certainly will keep in touch. We share a deep soul connection now, a bond of five-million steps. We are a community, a church of sorts; we will continue to be a *Band of Brothers*.

This will be my last journal entry since I am just a short drive and then flight from seeing my family. After I see them, I will not be writing. Someday, I will compile this journal into a book. But for now, my time will be theirs alone without the distractions. My journaling is over.

The trail taught me what it had to teach me. I entered fifty pounds' overweight, out of shape, and unable to maintain my peace of mind. I left the trail with fifty pounds or so less body fat, stronger than ever, and in complete control of my inner peace and strength.

To my wife, who suffered years along with me and my "gift", I want her to know these five-million difficult steps I have taken made all things new. The words of the classic Blues Brother's song come to mind:

Got what I got the hard way
And I'll make it better,
each and every day.
So honey, don't you fret
Cause you ain't seen nothing yet
I'm a Soul Man
I'm a Soul Man
I'm a Soul Man
I'm a Soul Man

I have fully assimilated my "disability" into a valuable "gift" that I will have access to at all times, 24-7 since positive energy is from God, and I am - and will always be - aware of His presence. I will never be weakened; I will always remain strong. I have become the "Soul Man"

So in conclusion, if I have one last insight to offer our nation, it would be this:

We are all conduits between the visible and the invisible; the physical and the spiritual worlds. Life's biggest worries seem to manifest from the separation of the two, yet all problems can be solved in their union. When we see our physical world through a spiritual lens, the puzzle pieces seem to fit together perfectly. We learn to harmonize with the ebb and flow of life. We experience peace of mind, body, and spirit. We discover God is with us on the journey as a travel companion, teaching us, quieting us, and revealing to us His grace. And, His grace is sufficient.

(9:11 p.m., still 1st day off the trail)

I was not going to write again, but the airplane pilot just said we are preparing for landing. That means I am just a few minutes from seeing my wife and family who will be picking me up at the airport. I am beside myself with excitement. I will be seeing the people who matter most to me after I land. It has been 168 days! We spoke on the phone at every town along the trail, but I am finally going to see them. I missed them terribly. I can't believe it. I am speechless.

Life is good.

God is good.

I just felt like I had to say that before I put this journal away for good.

One final thought

It has been over ten years since I hiked the entire Appalachian Trail and all is just as it should be. My family is doing well. My three children are off on their own finding their value in the world. My wife and I have an empty nest. We still hit the trail together as a family one week out of every summer. Each week continues to teach us something. God walks with us; all the while, He is teaching us, quieting us, and revealing His grace to us.

My life has changed for the better in 2003. I have kept my peace of mind and my health ever since. My body weight has been the same since the day I stepped off the trail. I attribute it all to the spiritual lens I have been looking through since the trail.

You make healthy, mindful choices regarding your health when you are influenced by only positive energy; you choose healthy relationships; you refuse harmful substances; you chose to share kindness; you choose to eat foods that will nourish you; you care for Mother Nature; and, you choose to take active steps away from a sedentary lifestyle. The health of body and soul is our choice. It is a choice I gladly make every day.

I have been using my gift. There is not a day goes by when I find I can sooth the soul of someone who is troubled. Since I continued my work as both a chaplain and a physical therapist after the trail, I have unlimited opportunities to make life better for people I am in contact with every day at the senior community where I am employed.

Yesterday, I spent time with a man who has been a living nightmare for our nursing staff. He was radiating with negative energy when I went in his room. I felt it. Thanks to my mastery of my superpower, I politely declined getting caught in the vortex of negativity that was affecting the staff.

The doctor told this man he will be dying soon.

He told me about his childhood, the teenage years, the military service, his career, his business. He shared all of these things quite freely.

He was divorced twice and now is married to a woman who is much younger. He thinks she is disinterested in his recovery because of the "millions" she will get from his estate when he is gone.

As he talked, he was becoming tolerant of me. I could feel his energy change. He liked talking about his life. Then he slipped and said something about his son dying and then he immediately stopped talking. I could feel his energy change to negative once again.

"Get out of here, I said too much!"

I did not leave. I just sat, offering him an ear and my peace of mind.

After cursing me a few times for not leaving, he eventually shared with me that fifty years ago, his teenage son was killed on a motorcycle that he purchased for him. This man's world started to come unraveled after that moment. He became embittered. He started to find fault with other family members. Separations, divorces, estranged surviving children and grandchildren; each year he became more isolated and angry. Fifty years later, I sit next to him as he lay lamenting on his final bedrest.

I let him talk for better than an hour. He shouted. He cried. He cursed. He sobbed. Eventually, after wearing himself out with emotions he turned to me and asked: *was my whole life wrong?*

I was silent. Because I knew, at some level, his life was wrong. He caused the isolation. He caused the pain in his family's life: the divorces, the estranged surviving children, and the grandchildren.

He chose the negative energy. But, on another level, he did not understand the condition of his soul. He railed against God and the world for the guilt he felt after the loss of his son who died while riding the motorcycle he purchased. It was his greatest tragedy. It was a double tragedy. It claimed the life of a son, but it also claimed a long life of a father who could not see any grace anywhere after that day fifty years ago. The souls of family members were scattered about for the generations that followed. They were caught in his wake of negative energy. He needed a soul repair; He never took the necessary steps to heal. All negative energy. Everyone suffered.

I am doing what I can. I will visit him every day while he is living. I want a happy ending for him, his wife, his estranged children, and his grandchildren. There would be no greater gift to the man and his family than to break the cycle of negative energy, in order to start seeing God' s grace again. I hope we will have enough time to assemble all the family's scattered puzzle pieces before it is too late.

Don't force the pieces together. If it doesn't seem to fit, remain calm and try a different piece. It eventually all fits together as designed. Trust the designer... If only this man heard this fifty years ago as he was trying to reassemble his scattered life after the tragic death of his son, so much pain would have been avoided.

You have read my journal from many years ago when I chose to hike the entire Appalachian Trail. Along the journey, I learned life's puzzle pieces fit together perfectly. That seems to be how it works on a long journey of physical exertion coupled with deep spiritual contemplation; your rhythmic movement of your body allows your mind to go on autopilot and you get lost in meditation for months on end. Wisdom flows to you with great clarity if you allow the *busyness* of thought to subside and the *still small voice* of God to speak through the silence.

Along the journey, I morphed into the "Soul Man". I know how it happened. It's complicated. There were five-million difficult steps. But, I thought of a riddle that might help explain it in simple terms:

The anxious attendee of the spiritual retreat asked the minister, "why can't I find God?"

The minister replied, "because you are trying too hard."

To this, the attendee complained, "I might as well quit trying and just go for a long walk in the woods."

The minister countered "Ah, I believe you will finally find Who you are looking for."

It is really finished!
Grace and Peace to you always,
thanks for reading,
Soul Man

Aging Grace
The Journey to
a Healthy 100

Explore the "thin place" where the physical and the spiritual worlds are paper thin. Discover the life patterns of real people, who have loved 100 healthy and inspired years of living.

www.tomhafer.com

Soul Man
Five-Million Difficult Steps to
Spiritual and Physical Health

One troubled soul hiked 2,200 miles on the Appalachian Trail. His five-million difficult contemplative steps taught him how to harmonize with the peaks and the valleys of the path. He learned the biggest problems have only spiritual solutions. Entering the woods in Georgia out of shape and hopeless, this troubled soul emerged from Maine six months later transformed in body and spirit. He returned home a hero of sorts, with the wisdom to heal a nation, one troubled soul at a time.

www.tomhafer.com

To Recieve
Pastor's Weekly Ramble
visit
www.tomhafer.com

Pastor's Weekly Ramble

Life becomes a spiritual journey when we lose the notion that we are on a frantic foot race to discover God. Once we walk away from the "busy-ness" of our search for discovery - once the dust settles - we become aware of God's presence. We see clearly we were not racing to find Him in some heavenly future, God was and continues to be our travel companion in the present. This spiritual awareness allows us to quiet our minds regardless of the distractions and negative energies that surround us. We walk *with* and not *to* God. We maintain inner peace.

www.tomhafer.com

To Recieve
Pastor's Weekly Ramble
visit
www.tomhafer.com

Pastor's Weekly Ramble

When we find ourselves at peace with our world, we see that there is no need for alcohol or drugs, or pity, or comfort food, or destructive relationships, or guilt, or shame. In every case - with inner peace - the scars of the past remain in the past, and the promising future relies on the decisions we make while in our present peace of mind.

www.tomhafer.com

To Recieve
Pastor's Weekly Ramble
visit
www.tomhafer.com

Pastor's Weekly Ramble

*When the shoe fits,
you forget it is on.*

*When the soul is at
peace, you forget it
was ever restless.*

*Be Still and know
that I am God.*
(Psalm 46:10)

www.tomhafer.com

Printed in the United States
By Bookmasters